Alfred's Premier Piano Course

POP AND MOVIE

W0009372

Dennis Alexander • Gayle Kowalchyk • E. L. Lancaster • Victoria McArthur • Martha Mier

Alfred's *Premier Piano Course* Pop and Movie Hits 1A includes familiar pieces that reinforce concepts included in Lesson Book 1A. The music continues the strong pedagogical focus of the course while providing the enjoyment of playing familiar music. Duet accompaniments create rich sounds and can aid the student with rhythmic security. Both solo and duet parts contain measure numbers for easy reference.

The pieces in this book correlate page-by-page with the materials in Lesson Book 1A. They should be assigned according to the instructions in the upper right corner of each page of this book. They also may be assigned as review material at any time after the student has passed the designated Lesson Book page. Pop and Movie Hits 1A also can be used to supplement any beginning piano method.

Allowing students to study music they enjoy is highly motivating. Consequently, reading and rhythm skills often improve greatly when studying pop and movie music. The authors hope that the music in Pop and Movie Hits 1A brings hours of enjoyment.

Edited by Morton Manus

Produced by
Alfred Music Publishing Co., Inc.
P.O. Box 10003
Van Nuys, CA 91410-0003
alfred.com

Printed in USA.

ISBN-10: 0-7390-6495-9
ISBN-13: 978-0-7390-6495-5

CONTENTS

The Trolley Song

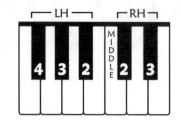

The Trolley Song was sung by Judy Garland in the 1944 film Meet Me in St. Louis. This movie musical tells the story of four sisters who lived in St. Louis at the time of the 1904 Louisiana Purchase World Exposition. Judy Garland also sang the popular favorite "Have Yourself a Merry Little Christmas" in this movie. Both songs became famous musical standards.

Words and Music by
Hugh Martin and Ralph Blane

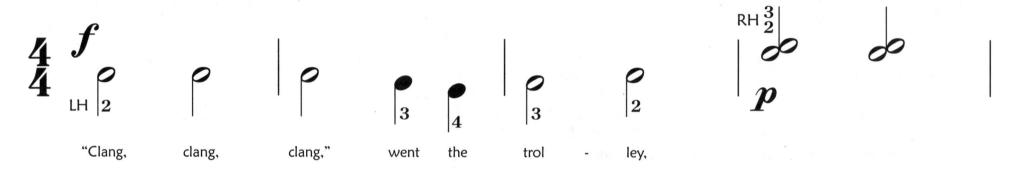

"Clang, clang, clang," went the trol - ley,

Duet: Student plays one octave higher.

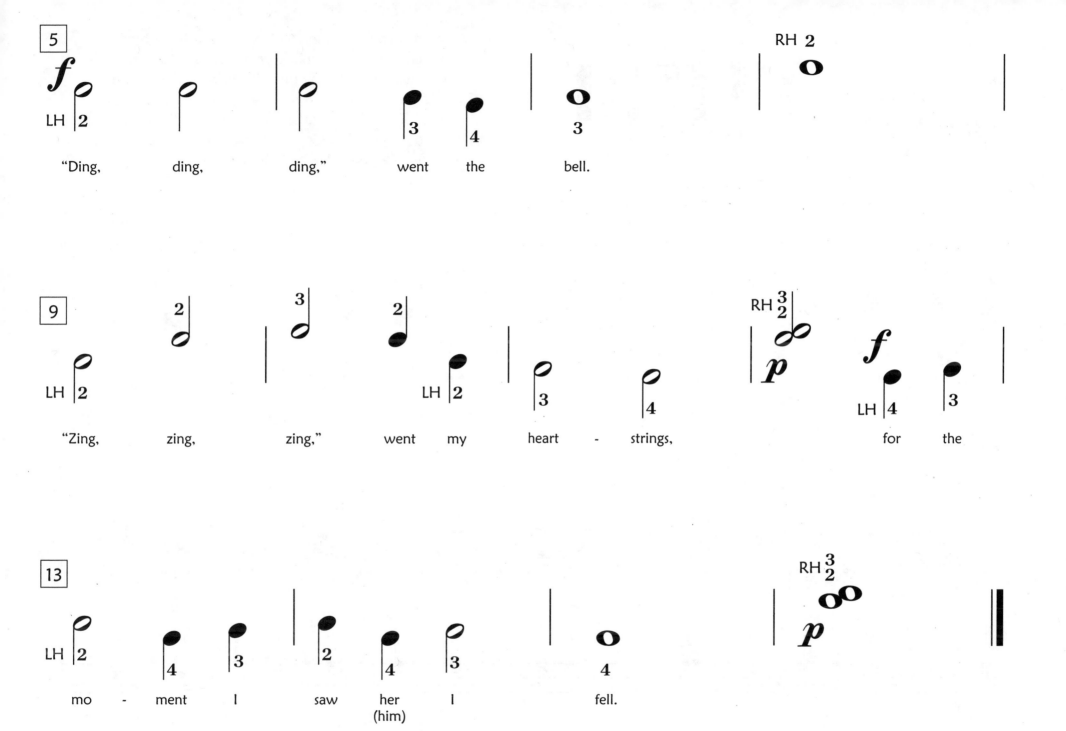

Bye, Bye Blackbird

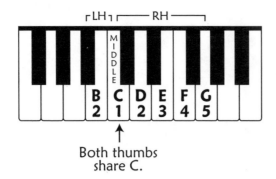

Both thumbs
share C.

Words by Mort Dixon
Music by Ray Henderson

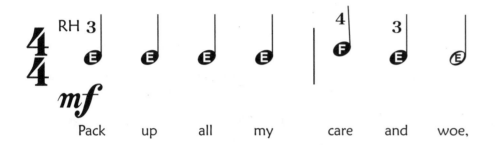

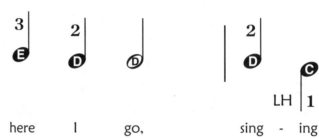

Pack   up   all   my   care   and   woe,   here   I   go,   sing - ing   low,

Duet: Student plays one octave higher.

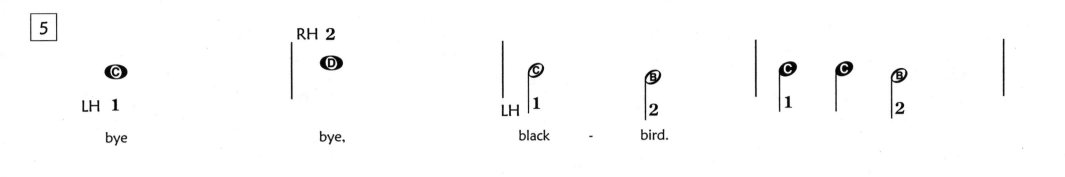

bye   bye,   black - bird.

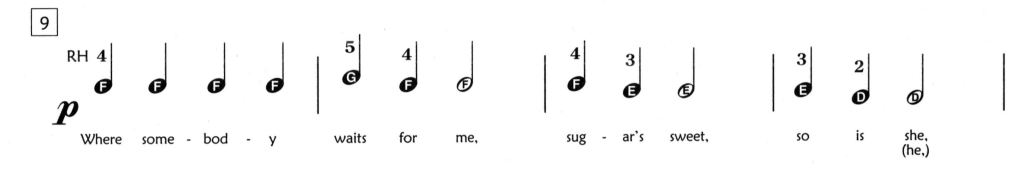

Where some - bod - y   waits for me,   sug - ar's sweet,   so   is   she,
(he,)

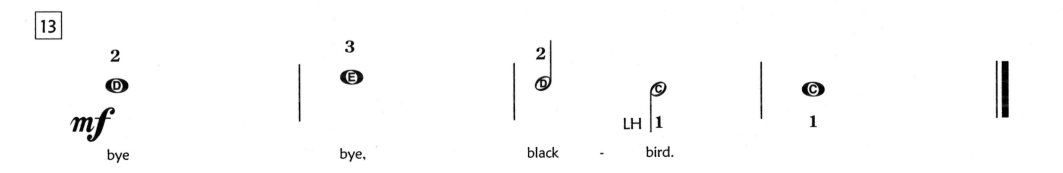

bye   bye,   black - bird.

Mickey Mouse March

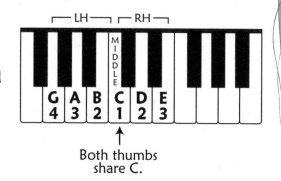

Both thumbs
share C.

Words and Music by
Jimmie Dodd

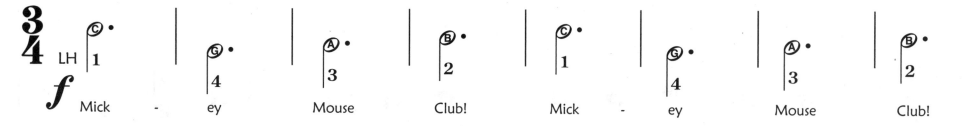

Mick - ey   Mouse   Club!   Mick - ey   Mouse   Club!

Duet: Student plays one octave higher.

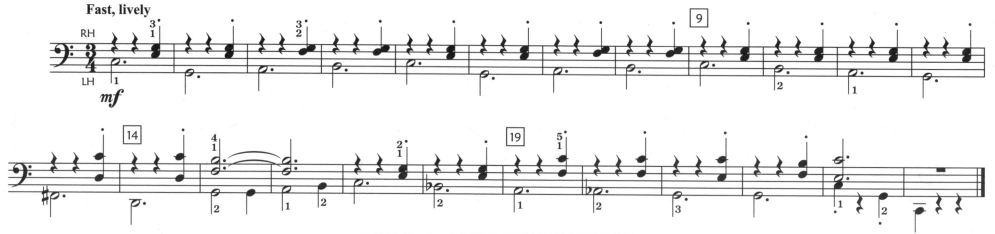

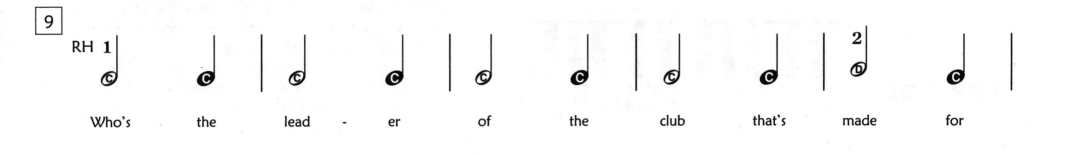

9

RH **1**

Who's   the   lead -   er   of   the   club   that's   made   for

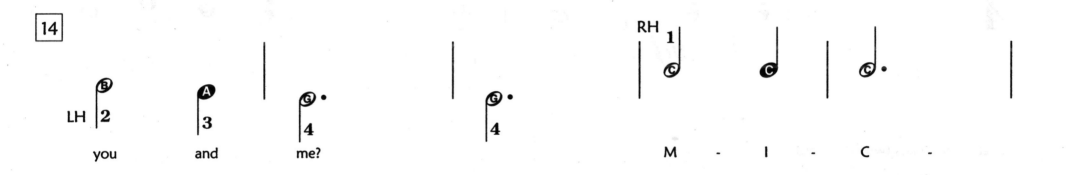

14

LH **2**   **3**   **4**   **4**   RH **1**

you   and   me?   M -   I -   C -

19   RH **3**   **1**   **2**

LH **1**   LH **2**   **1**   **4**   **1**

K -   E -   Y   M -   O -   U -   S -   E!

The Rose

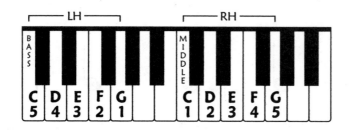

The Rose *was made famous by Bette Midler in the 1979 movie of the same name. The movie was loosely based on the life of the 1960s legendary rock star, Janis Joplin. It tells the story of her struggles in dealing with a demanding career. Bette Midler received an Academy Award nomination for Best Actress for her role in the movie.*

Words and Music by
Amanda McBroom

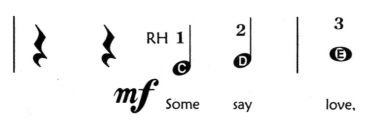

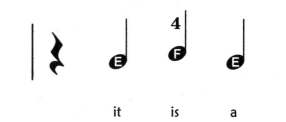

mf Some say love, it is a

Duet: Student plays **two** octaves higher.

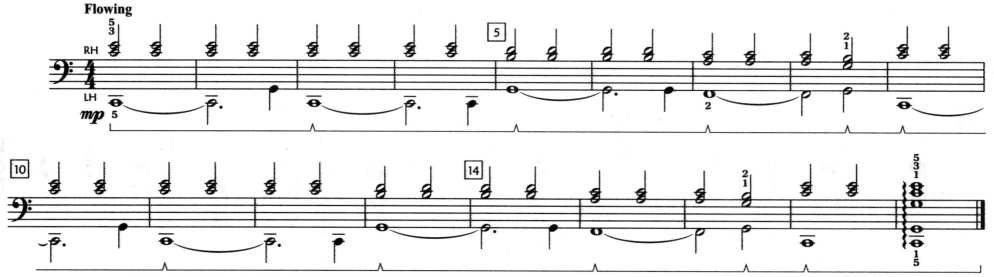

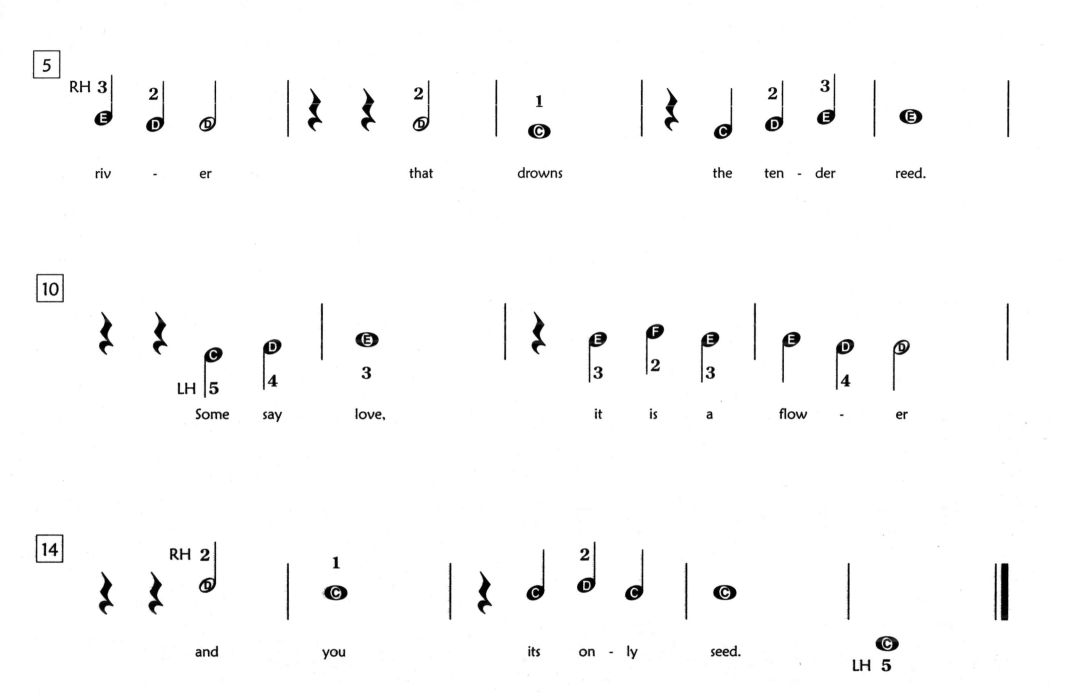

Whistle While You Work
(Left Hand)

Words by Larry Morey
Music by Frank Churchill

The 1937 film Snow White and the Seven Dwarfs was the first animated full-length movie, the first film produced in color, and the first film made by Walt Disney Productions. **Whistle While You Work** is one of the many famous songs from the soundtrack. Over the years, it has been used in many TV shows and other movies.

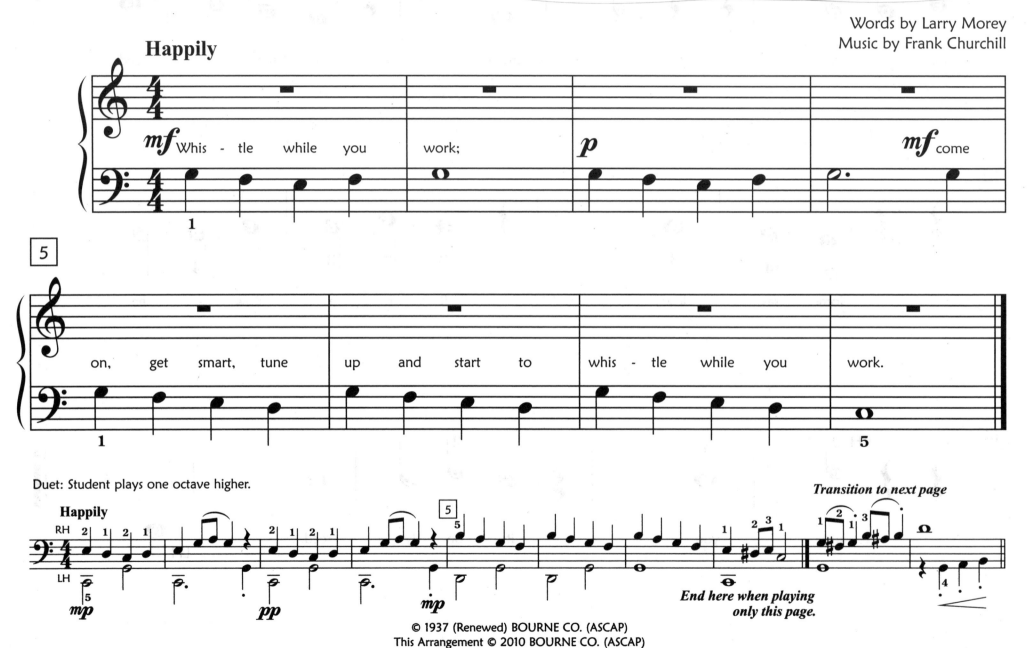

Duet: Student plays one octave higher.

Transition to next page

End here when playing only this page.

Whistle While You Work
(Right Hand)

Words by Larry Morey
Music by Frank Churchill

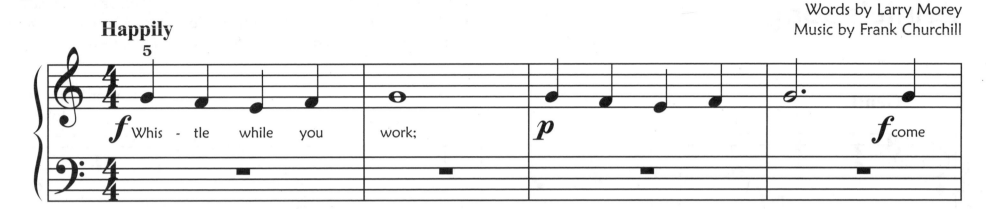

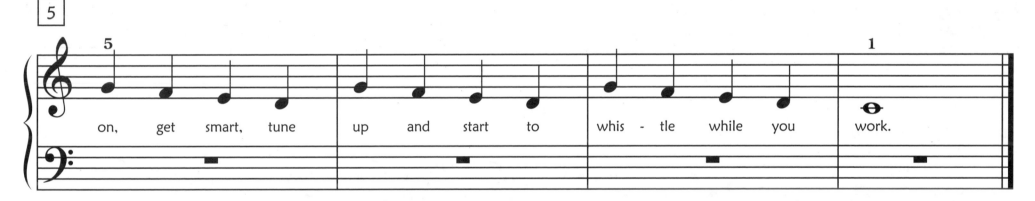

Premier Performer

For a longer performance when playing with duet part:
1. Play *Whistle While You Work* on page 10.
2. Teacher plays the two-measure transition on page 10.
3. Play *Whistle While You Work* on page 11.

Duet: Student plays one octave higher.

Annie's Song

John Denver was one of the most popular singers and songwriters of the 1970s. The concept for **Annie's Song** was developed by Denver while riding on a ski lift up Bell Mountain in Aspen, Colorado. Denver was overwhelmed by the beauty of the mountains which made him think of his wife, Annie. Released in 1974, Annie's Song has become a favorite song recorded by many artists and is frequently sung at weddings.

Words and Music by
John Denver

Gently

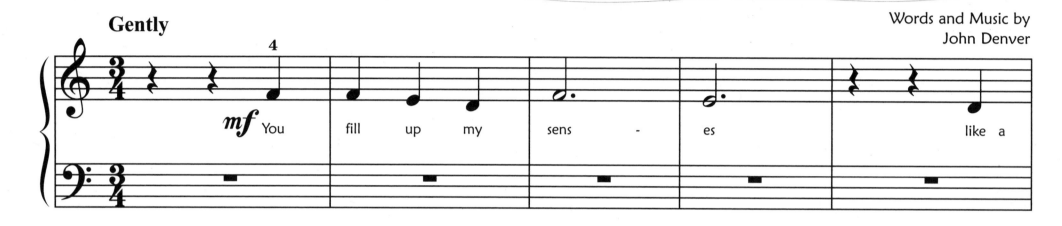

You fill up my sens - es like a

Duet: Student plays one octave higher.

Gently

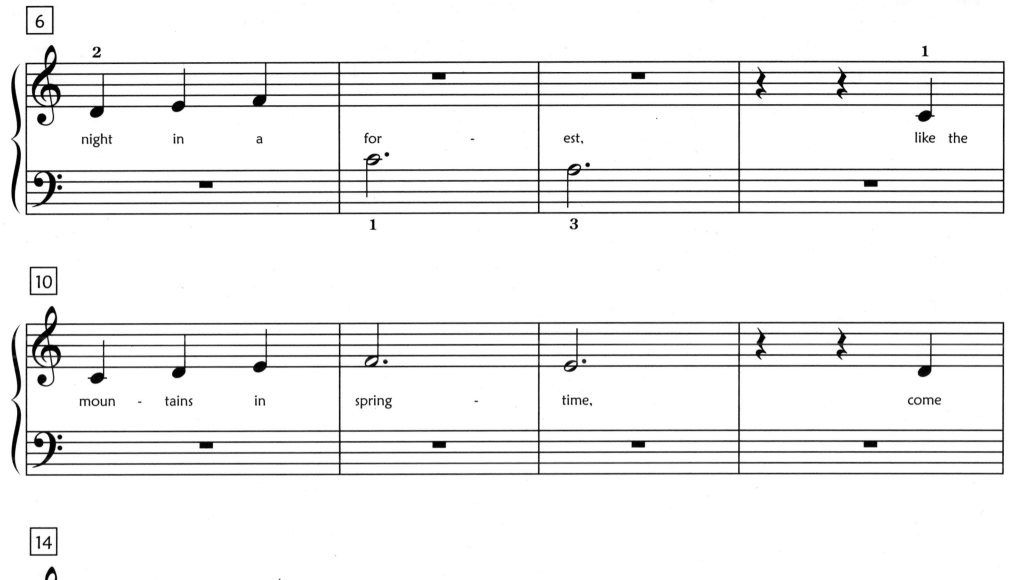
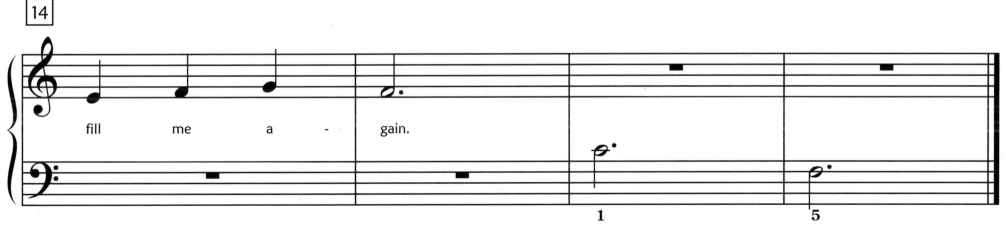

Scooby Doo, Where Are You?

Scooby Doo, Where Are You? has continued to be a popular cartoon series since its beginning in 1969. The original theme song had no lyric and was only instrumental. The vocal Scooby Doo, Where Are You? was recorded three days before the premiere of the show!

Words and Music by
David Mook and Ben Raleigh

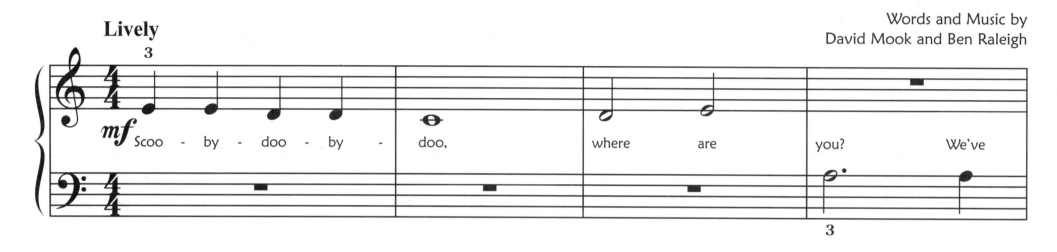

Scoo - by - doo - by - doo, where are you? We've

Duet: Student plays one octave higher.

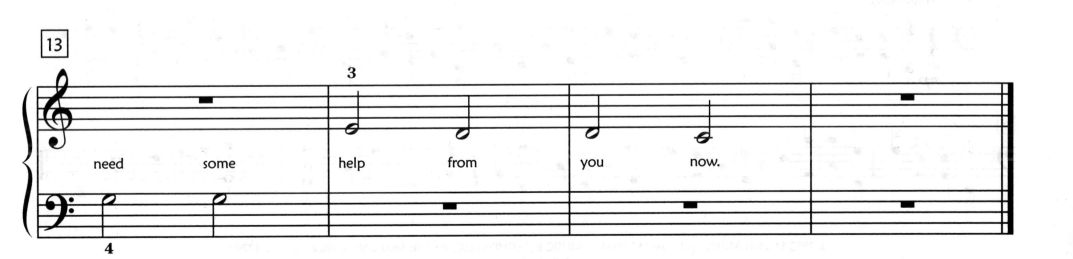

Up Where We Belong

Up Where We Belong is a song from the 1986 film An Officer and a Gentleman. The producer originally complained about the song and wanted to take it out of the movie. However, it eventually became a No. 1 hit on the Billboard charts and won the Grammy award for Best Song in 1986.

Words by Will Jennings
Music by Jack Nitzsche and Buffy Sainte-Marie

mf Love lift us up where we be - long, where the

Duet: Student plays one octave higher.

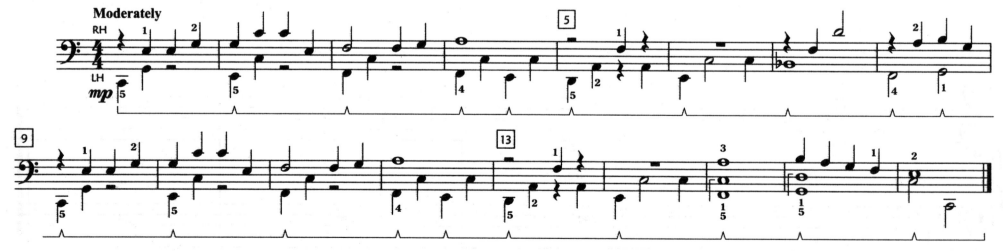

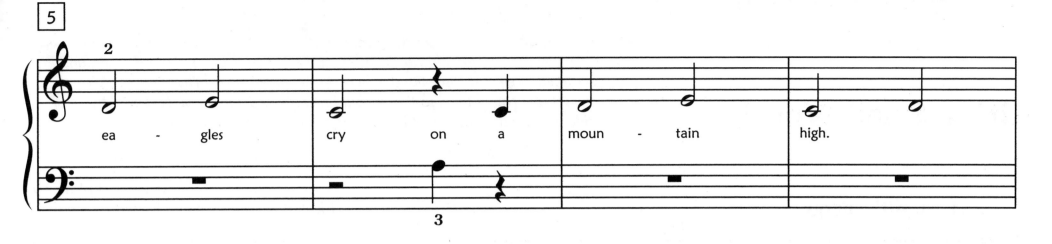

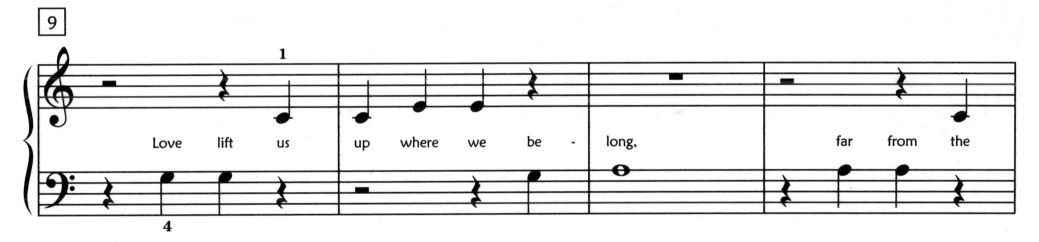

It's a Small World

It's a Small World was written as a theme song for the ride with the same name at Disney Parks. The ride was featured at the 1964 New York World's Fair, and was then moved to Disneyland, where it opened in 1966. The Shermans wrote the song in round form so that it could be repeated continuously during the ride without the riders' hearing unpleasant dissonances (musical clashes).

Words and Music by
Richard M. Sherman and Robert B. Sherman

Fast, with energy

Duet: Student plays one octave higher.

it's a small world af - ter all,

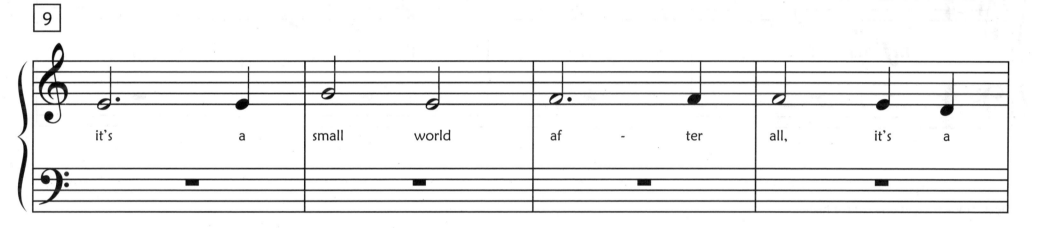

it's a small world af - ter all, it's a

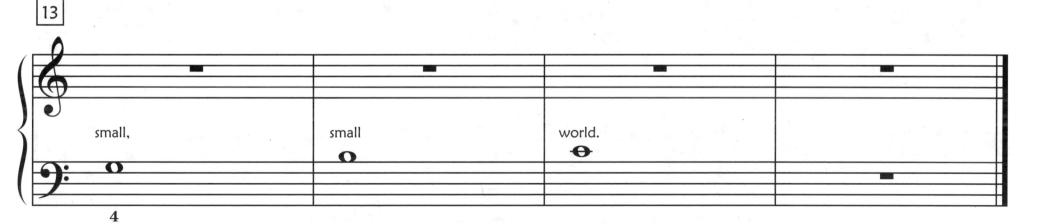

small, small world.

This Land Is Your Land

This Land Is Your Land, written by Woody Guthrie in the 1940s, is one of the most lasting folk songs in our country's history. When Guthrie wrote the song, some say he had grown tired of repeatedly hearing Irving Berlin's "God Bless America," and he decided to write his own patriotic song. Pop legend Bruce Springstein said it is "one of the most beautiful songs ever written."

Words and Music by
Woodie Guthrie

Cheerfully

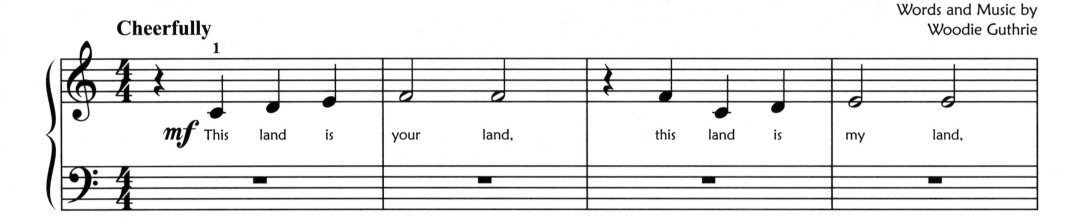

mf This land is your land, this land is my land,

Duet: Student plays one octave higher.

Cheerfully

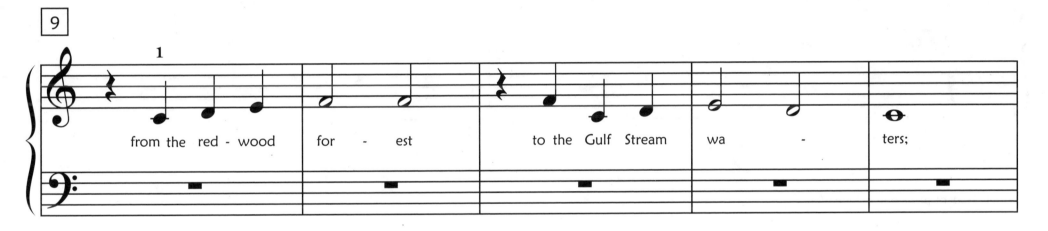

This Is It!

The Bugs Bunny Show was a hit animated cartoon series shown on television in many different formats for 40 years. The theme song **This Is It!** is sung by Bugs Bunny and Daffy Duck in unison. For the final chorus, they are joined by other Looney Tunes/Merrie Melodies characters.

Words and Music by
Mack David and Jerry Livingston

With energy

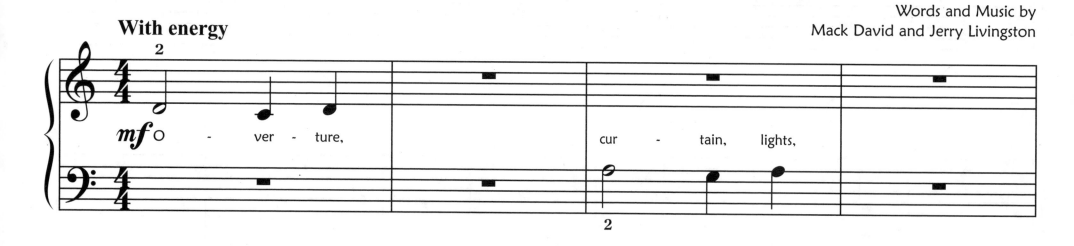

Duet: Student plays one octave higher.

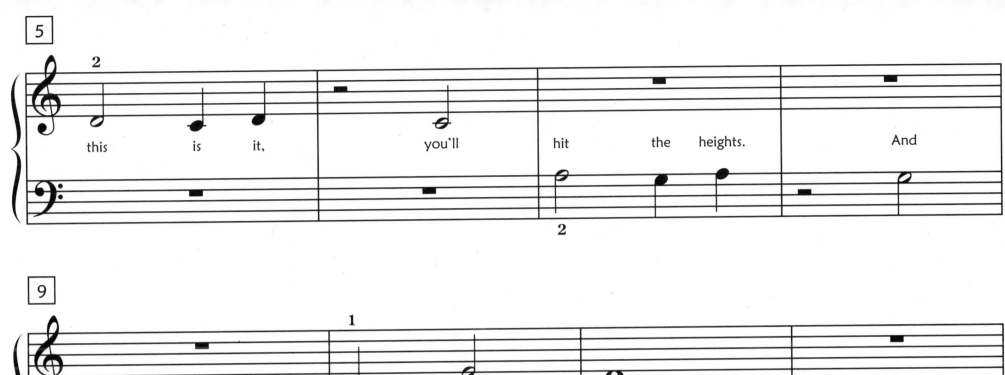

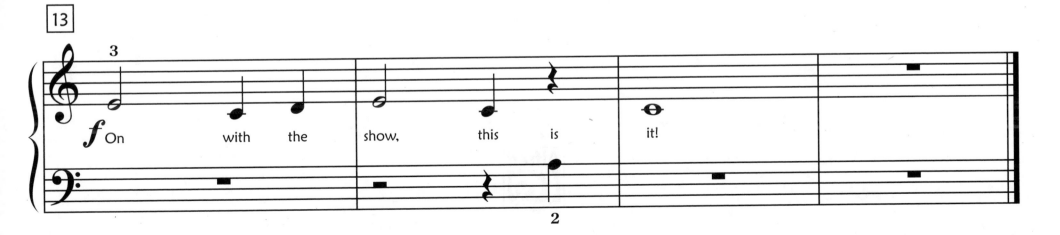